Basketball Belles

How Two Teams and One Scrappy Player Put Women's Hoops on the Map

by Sue Macy

illustrated by Matt Collins

Holiday House / New York

Nobody can ever accuse me of being a girly-girl. Sure, I can sashay around in a ruffled skirt carrying a parasol if I have to. But I'm a lot more comfortable in breeches and spurs. My name is Agnes Morley. I grew up working on my family's ranch in New Mexico. Getting dirty came with the territory.

My mother hoped sending me to Stanford University would make me a lady. What would she say if she saw me now, hurrying through the streets of San Francisco to play basketball? I'm sure she'd prefer that I was going to tea on the arm of a handsome gentleman.

Not today. In fact, there will be no gentlemen at the game. Our opponents from Berkeley don't feel it's proper for women to perspire in front of men. I think that's silly. At Stanford we play our games outdoors, where anyone can see.

Some people feel women shouldn't play basketball at all. The game, of course, was designed for men. Then Senda Berenson, a teacher at Smith College in Massachusetts, adapted the rules to make it less rough for women. One thing she did was draw lines that divide the court into three sections. Women are assigned to a section, and they have to stay there. In the men's game, players are allowed to run all over the court.

I don't think anyone knows what to expect today. After all, this will be the first basketball game ever played between two women's college teams.

More than five hundred ladies cheering at the top of their lungs welcome us into the arena. Actually, their behavior is anything but ladylike. The last time I heard such a roar, I was caught in a cattle stampede!

As we take our positions, I block out the noise and study our opponents. It worries me that the Berkeley players are taller and heavier than we are. Out on the range, I've held my own against antelope and coyotes and even grizzly bears. But as a guard on our team, I'll have to stand up to three sturdy forwards charging their basket. Can I do it? It's time to find out.

A hush falls over the crowd as the referee tosses the big, stuffed, leather ball in the air to start the game. I stand alert, ready any time the sphere comes toward me. When I catch it, I whip it to Stella in the center of the court. She throws it to our forwards so one of them can shoot at our basket.

Sometimes, though, my opponents are too quick. Over and over, I find myself pushed onto the hard floor in a scramble for the ball. My opponents and teammates dive on top of me, and I am crushed under their weight. If women's basketball is a tamer version of the men's game, I'd hate to see how men play!

Most of the action in the first half is across the court, near our team's basket. Midway through the half, Stella throws the ball to Mattie, one of our forwards. She takes a long shot.

Mattie's ball sails right in. We're ahead, 1–0.
We have the advantage now. Two swift passes
bring the ball into the hands of my teammate
Frances. But her shot misses. Worse, it knocks the
basket off-kilter. We have no choice but to get the janitor
and his assistant to fix it.

Out they come, the only men in the building. The assistant stares at us so intently, he almost knocks the janitor off his ladder! When the basket is secured, the two men make a hasty exit.

With the ball back in play, the momentum shifts. Berkeley's captain throws a stinging pass to one of her forwards. She launches a shot that lands right in the basket. We are tied, 1–1. For the rest of the first half, we try mightily to break the deadlock. But no one else scores.

Berkeley comes back from the halftime break with even more energy. It seems that the ball is always whizzing around me as our opponents push to their basket. My teammates and I jump and lunge to stop all of their shots.

Berkeley's guards play just as fiercely around our basket, and neither team scores. Suddenly a piercing whistle stops the action. In our frenzied activity, both teams have committed fouls. Now one player from each team gets to take a foul shot.

One of Berkeley's forwards steps
up to shoot. I watch helplessly. The
rules forbid us from blocking foul shots.
"Go, Edith!" someone yells from the stands.
She closes her eyes for just a second, as if to see
the shot in her mind. Then she heaves the ball. It
sails through the air . . .

and misses. Frances steps up for our team. The arena is so quiet I can hear the wind rustling the American flag outside. Frances turns the ball around in her hands before launching it with terrific force. It flies toward the basket . . .

and drops right in. We are ahead, 2–1. Our fans cheer wildly. The Berkeley faithful shout for their team to pull even. We struggle to keep them off balance, determined that Stanford will win the battle this day. Finally, time runs out.

Victory is ours! We laugh and hug one another, beside ourselves with joy. We even give a cheer for the other team, and they for us. What a sight we all are! Our hair is messy. Our bloomers are torn. Our faces are streaked with sweat. This might not be what my mother had in mind when she sent me to Stanford to become a lady. But I think that a lady can be tough and strong as well as refined and polite. She can even play basketball.

Author's Note

Agnes Morley really did play guard for Stanford University in that historic basketball game on April 4, 1896. Almost every account of the forty-minute game praised the power and accuracy of her passes. The *San Francisco Chronicle* said, "Miss Morley of Stanford did some admirable work in the second half, with a long, fine, straight throw, clean from the shoulder, as though a man and not a girl were flinging the sphere." According to the *San Francisco Examiner*, Agnes also was the player who recounted the highlights of the game for her classmates when the team returned to Stanford. (The game had been played at the Page Street Armory in San Francisco, a neutral site between Berkeley and Stanford.) That, as well as her intriguing personal background, made her the perfect player to focus on in this story.

All of the details about Agnes's childhood in New Mexico are true. After graduating from Stanford in 1899 with a degree in economics, she went on to become a successful writer and the mother of four children. In 1941, at age sixty-seven, Agnes published an award-winning memoir titled *No Life for a Lady*. This book, which looks back at her life growing up in New Mexico, was called "the richest chronicle of Western life from a woman's point of view" by *The New York Times*. Agnes lived much of her adult life away from New Mexico, but she returned there after the death of her husband in 1944. She died at her ranch in 1958 at age eighty-three.

Agnes is not the only player from the 1896 basketball game who went on to achieve great things. Two of the women from Stanford's opponents—the University of California at Berkeley—became medical doctors, and one became a nurse. Another became a college professor and an expert on plant science. At least two Stanford players became teachers, including Frances Tucker, who scored the game's winning basket. Many of the women also married and gave birth to future athletes. Stanford's captain, Stella McCray, had three sons who became sports stars at the university. Agnes Morley's son, Norman Cleaveland, won a gold medal in rugby at the 1924 Olympic Games.

Women's basketball continued to grow in the twentieth century, though early on, intercollegiate play was limited by physical educators who worried that female athletes would push themselves too hard in the quest for victory. The Olympics added the women's game as a medal sport in 1976; and in the 1980s and 1990s, women's college ball entered the big-time. Powerhouse teams from the universities of Tennessee and Connecticut built dynasties, and an ever-expanding roster of challengers—including Stanford—vied for championship titles. One hundred years after the contest portrayed in this book, a U.S. gold medal at the 1996 Olympics led to the formation of two women's professional leagues, including the WNBA. Fittingly, during its initial years, no school sent more players to the WNBA than Stanford.

Timeline of Women's Basketball

1891 James Naismith invents basketball in Springfield, Massachusetts.

1892 Senda Berenson, a teacher at Smith College in Massachusetts, adapts the rules of basketball for women.

1896 Stanford and Berkeley play the first women's intercollegiate game.

1901 Senda Berenson edits the first official book of rules for the women's game.

1913 New rules allow a one-bounce dribble.

1918 Baskets with open bottoms officially replace those with closed bottoms and pull chains.

1932 All baskets now count as two points instead of one.

1938 Women officially begin playing on a court divided into halves instead of thirds, with six players per team.

1949 Two-bounce dribbles are introduced for women.

1961 Three-bounce dribbles are allowed.

1966 Unlimited dribbles are allowed.

1969 The first national college basketball championships for women take place.

1971 Women officially adopt the full-court game, with five players per team.

1972 President Richard Nixon signs Title IX of the 1972 Education Amendments into law. It outlaws gender discrimination in schools that receive federal funds.

1973 Colleges award basketball scholarships to women for the first time.

1976 Basketball becomes a medal sport for women at the Summer Olympics.

1978 The professional Women's Basketball League (WBL) is formed. It folds in 1981.

1987 The three-point shot is introduced for women.

1990 Stanford wins its first national women's basketball title.

1996 The professional American Basketball League (ABL) begins. It folds in 1998.

1997 The Women's National Basketball Association (WNBA) pro league begins.

Stanford's Ada Edwards, one of the umpires at the 1896 game.

Resources

Books

A Century of Women's Basketball: From Frailty to Final Four edited by Joan S. Hult and Marianna Trekell (Reston, VA: National Association for Girls and Women in Sport, 1991). This collection of academic articles covers the development and evolution of the women's game from the 1890s through the 1980s.

Hoop Girlz by Lucy Jane Bledsoe (New York: Holiday House, 2002). Eleven-year-old River fills a girls' basketball team with second-string players and leads them to the finals of a local tournament.

J is for Jump Shot: A Basketball Alphabet by Michael Ulmer, illustrated by Mark Braught (Chelsea, MI: Sleeping Bear Press, 2005). Besides defining terms from *air* through *zone*, this book is packed with information about the rules and history of basketball.

No Life for a Lady by Agnes Morley Cleaveland (Lincoln, NB: University of Nebraska Press, 1977). Originally published in 1941. Agnes Morley's award-winning memoir focuses on her adventures growing up on her mother's ranch in western New Mexico in the late 1800s.

Slam Dunk by Donna King (Boston: Kingfisher, 2007). Ashlee, thirteen, defies her mother to attend a youth basketball camp that could be the first step to the pros.

Swish! by Bill Martin Jr. & Michael Sampson, illustrated by Michael Chesworth (New York: Holt, 1997). Illustrations and text tell the story of the final minute of a championship basketball game between two girls' teams.

Places to Visit

Naismith Memorial Basketball Hall of Fame
1000 West Columbus Avenue
Springfield, Massachusetts 01105
413-781-6500
www.hoophall.com

This state-of-the-art interactive museum commemorates the game's top male and female players, coaches, and teams, and also gives visitors a chance to test their reaction times, vertical leaps, and other basketball skills.

Women's Basketball Hall of Fame
700 Hall of Fame Drive
Knoxville, Tennessee 37915
865-633-9000
www.wbhof.com

Artifacts, photographs, scrapbooks, and videotapes bring the history of the women's game to life in this hall, which opened in 1999. There's also a basketball court where visitors can shoot at baskets from the past, present, and future.

Courtesy of Stanford University Archives

Agnes Morley is in the back row, third from the right, in this photograph
of the 1896 Stanford women's basketball team. Captain Stella McCray is at center,
holding what seems to be a football. According to Stanford's archivist, it wasn't
uncommon for early photographs of basketball teams to feature the wrong ball!

Acknowledgments

Writing this book has occupied my thoughts for close to a decade, so there are many people
to thank. First, my gratitude goes to Matt Collins for bringing this story to life with his
powerful, dynamic illustrations. Amanda Aikman helped with the research early on, and
editors Dianne Hess, Regina Griffin, and Mary Cash encouraged me along the way. Eleni
Beja and Pam Glauber inherited the task of nursing me through my transition to picture
book author, and they did so with extreme patience, impressive skill, and admirable tact.

None of this would have been possible without my agent, Ken Wright. My parents,
brother, friends, and relatives also offered unwavering support throughout the process.
Thanks especially to Sheila Wolinsky, who was there at the beginning, and to Jackie
Glasthal for crucial and invaluable feedback on the manuscript at every stage.

Special thanks go to the present-day women's basketball teams of Stanford and the
University of California at Berkeley and their coaches, Tara VanDerveer and Joanne
Boyle, respectively. It was a pleasure to get an inside look at today's teams and imagine
their counterparts on the court more than one hundred years ago.

This book is dedicated to Estelle Freedman, Edgar E. Robinson Professor in United
States History at Stanford, who sparked my interest in women's history several decades ago
at Princeton and continues to be an inspiring mentor and a treasured friend.

For Estelle
— S. M.

To Charlotte
— M. C.

HOLIDAY HOUSE is registered in the U.S. Patent and Trademark Office.
Printed and Bound in October 2010 at Kwong Fat Offset Co., Ltd., Dongguan City,
Quang Dong Province, China.
The text typeface is Bookman.
The artwork was created in Corel Painter.
www.holidayhouse.com
First Edition
1 3 5 7 9 10 8 6 4 2

Library of Congress Cataloging-in-Publication Data
Macy, Sue.
Basketball belles : how two teams and one scrappy player put women's hoops on the map / by Sue Macy ;
illustrated by Matt Collins. — 1st ed.
p. cm.
ISBN 978-0-8234-2163-3 (harcover)
1. Cleaveland, Agnes Morley, 1874-1958. 2. Basketball players—United States—
Biography—Juvenile literature. 3. Women basketball players—
United States—Biography—Juvenile literature. 4. Women pioneers—New Mexico—
Biography—Juvenile literature. I. Collins, Matt, ill. II. Title.
GV884.C6M34 2010
796.323092—dc22
[B]
2009042498